Han
for Feasts and Seasons

by
Glynn MacNiven-Johnston
& Raymond Edwards

All booklets are published thanks to the generous support of the members of the Catholic Truth Society

CATHOLIC TRUTH SOCIETY
PUBLISHERS TO THE HOLY SEE

Contents

Introduction 3

Advent 8

Immaculate Conception 16

Christmas 20

Epiphany 28

Annunciation 38

Easter 46

Pentecost 55

Sacred Heart 60

Transfiguration 68

Assumption 72

Exaltation of the Cross 78

Christ the King 86

All rights reserved. First published 2017 by The Incorporated Catholic Truth Society, 40-46 Harleyford Road London SE11 5AY Tel: 020 7640 0042 Fax: 020 7640 0046. © 2017 The Incorporated Catholic Truth Society.

ISBN 978 1 78469 127 1

Introduction

What is a novena?

A novena is a way of praying, often for a particular need or grace. It consists of a prayer or prayers said over nine days. The word *novena* is originally Latin, and means "in a group of nine".[1] This is because a novena lasts for nine consecutive days; on each day, there is a particular prayer to be said, or devotional practice to be made.

The original novena, the model for all the rest, is the nine days between Christ's Ascension and the descent of the Holy Spirit at Pentecost, when, as we read in the Acts of the Apostles, "all these [Apostles] joined in continuous prayer, together with several women, including Mary the mother of Jesus".[2] The Church still asks Christians to pray with particular intensity between these two feast days for the Holy Spirit to renew the Christian community.[3]

---

[1] The official Latin equivalent is *novendialis prex*, "nine days' prayer".
[2] Acts 1:14.
[3] In 1897 Pope Leo XIII asked that this practice, which was of long custom, should be celebrated by all Catholics worldwide. The official *Handbook of Indulgences* states that "a *partial indulgence* is granted the Christian faithful who devoutly take part in a publicly celebrated novena before the solemnity of Christmas, Pentecost, or the Immaculate Conception of the Blessed Virgin Mary" (3rd edition 1986, English edition 1991, par. 33 (p. 72 in the edition published by the Catholic Book Publishing Corporation of New York)).

There are many different sorts of novena; you can make a novena using any prayer you want: the main thing is to pray it regularly for nine days in a row. Nevertheless most people will make a novena using a prayer composed for the purpose. Some novena prayers are long, and may include litanies, or meditations; others are short. You can make a novena using the same prayer nine times, or nine different prayers, one for each day. There are no rules; what follows are only suggestions.

Many novenas (including those in the companion volumes *Handbook of Novenas to the Saints* (CTS, 2010) and *Handbook of Scriptural Novenas* (CTS, 2015)) ask the intercession of a particular saint or biblical figure for whatever our intention may be. As well as interceding (praying) on our behalf, the saints are also examples of how the Christian life has been lived. We can see in their lives examples of how embracing God's will for us, whatever our individual circumstances, always brings the grace and strength from God we need to do what he asks us. Biblical figures are slightly different. Scripture is a record of God's mighty deeds with his people, which are the pattern for his deeds with us today. These figures stand as examples to us in their ability to accept, often after a struggle, the action of God in their lives, and his will for them. This acceptance allowed their lives to assume a particular shape and conform to the providential pattern God intended. They are at the same time historical and exemplary.

These novenas are different again. They take for their theme not a particular person's witness to God's work in them, but some of the great feasts and seasons of the Christian year. When we pray in this way, we are placing ourselves within the great rhythm of the Church's journey within time. All time is Christian time; that is to say, since God began his journey with his people, and more so since he took our human condition on him in a physical way by being born of a woman (the great event we call the Incarnation), we experience God's work in us, his presence alongside and within us, through the medium of time. All times are one for God, to be sure: he is not bound by time in the same way that we are, and he sees and causes things in a way we cannot properly imagine, from the viewpoint of his simultaneous presence to all times and places (what, in religious language, we call his eternity); but he has chosen to make time, the ongoing progression of days and seasons that are both the same as what we have known before, and yet somehow always new. This time, then, he has made the vehicle and the means of our salvation - that is to say, the way through which we experience this world as his world, and our days lived in it as not meaningless or random but always charged with his presence.

The Church from its earliest days has discerned particular characters in certain times and days within the yearly round. Some of these are taken up from the Jewish tradition, from which Christianity was born; others express the new events and developments specific to Christianity. These seasonal characteristics are expressed in the different texture we experience in the Church's worship, its liturgy, throughout the year. Advent, Lent, Eastertide, the great feasts of Jesus's life and the life of his mother Mary: all have their own particular flavour, if you like, by which the Church opens to us some aspect of the life of Christ's body that is her own, and our own, and invites us to live this aspect of the Christian life in a particular way during this season or on this feast.

The primary way we are called to do this is through the public liturgy of the Church: the Eucharist, and the Divine Office (the breviary). By praying as the Church prays throughout the year, we can enter more fully into the various aspects of the Christian life - which is, no more and no less, the life of God-with-us. These novenas have been composed with the intention of helping us to enter into various liturgical times more consciously, and to bring our prayers of intercession - that is, when we pray for God to give us some particular thing or virtue or help, or in some especial need, for ourselves or for another - within the circle of the Church's year. All of our needs, let us remember, all the things we ask for and the events we may find difficult or baffling, all these things happen within time: and time is God's. Whenever we pray, we pray at a particular time, during some part of the Christian year; perhaps we may be helped to pray if we place our intercessions consciously within this cycle, which, day in and day out, maps and records and celebrates God's saving work with his people. The works he has done for our ancestors in the faith, he will do again for us; we have only to ask.

How to use this booklet

Each novena in this booklet reflects on a particular feast or season within the Church's year, and invites us to put our own needs in this context. Where possible, we have given short passages of Scripture for each day, followed by a reflection on some aspect of the feast or season, and then a prayer.

On each day of the novena, say these, and add your particular intention, if you have one; then say the *Our Father*, the *Hail Mary*, and the *Glory Be*. Do this on each of the nine days.

You may find it helpful to keep a short time of silence after reading the passage from Scripture. Scripture is the Word of God; God speaks to us through it. But to hear what he wants to say to us, we need to be quiet and listen. We may have much to say to God; he surely has something to say to us.

Advent

On the last days of Advent, the Church turns our eyes and hearts to the coming of Christ in an especially focussed way. One means of doing this is by what are known as the "O Antiphons". This is not some obscure Irish family, but a series of seven short scriptural sentences that the Church uses as part of Vespers (Evening Prayer) between the 17th and 23rd of December. Each announces one of the names of Jesus, who is called Christ. We can make our prayer at this time in light of these names.

Light and darkness are very frequently mentioned in these texts. Our condition is seen as one sunk in darkness, without light, without hope, bound in prison in the depths of a night without dawn. This may not be our own experience, not now at any rate; but we will probably have at some point in our lives felt like this, or known someone who has. Darkness and captivity can take many forms; all can crush the spirit. From all of these, the light of Jesus Christ, small and weak in the form of a new-born baby (and new-born babies are very small, and very vulnerable), will set us free: for even the smallest light is stronger than darkness, which flees away from it. God is stronger than death. We need only ask.

First Day: O Sapientia (17th December)

O Wisdom, you come forth from the mouth of the Most High. You fill the universe and hold all things together in a strong yet gentle manner. O come to teach us the way to truth.

The last-written books of the Old Testament - the prophet Baruch, the Book of Wisdom - speak often of the Wisdom of God. This is a mysterious figure, often personified as a woman, who is a tangible presence of God in our world, who knows and understands all things, who can guide us, and guard us with her glory. The Prologue of St John's Gospel takes this enigmatic figure and identifies it with Jesus, the man who was born in Bethlehem and grew up in Nazareth, and who was anointed as the one to save God's people from their sins. The Greek word used is *Logos*, which is usually translated "Word", but means something far richer and more complex in the Greek philosophy of its time: an overmastering pattern, the very matrix of all things, by which all things are created and sustained, which enfolds and encompasses all things (Chinese thought speaks of the Tao in comparable terms). This is what is born in Jesus: the primordial pattern and vessel of all things, something as gentle as water and as stupendous as the starlit sky at night. We are called to bring his very life and being into our lives and selves.

❖ Father, help me to know you and follow you.
I ask you especially for *[here name your intention]*
Our Father - Hail Mary - Glory Be

Second Day: O Adonai (18th December)

O Adonai and leader of Israel, you appeared to Moses in a burning bush and you gave him the Law on Sinai. O come and save us with your mighty power.

This identifies the coming Christ with the deliverer God of the Hebrew Scriptures: Adonai, the Lord God who with mighty hand and outstretched arm opened the Red Sea to the children of Israel, and will open for us a way through all that bars our way, even death itself.

❖ Father, help me to believe you have power over all things.
I ask you especially for *[here name your intention]*
Our Father - Hail Mary - Glory Be

Third Day: O Radix Jesse (19th December)

O stock of Jesse, you stand as a signal for the nations; kings fall silent before you whom the peoples acclaim. O come to deliver us, and do not delay.

The royal house of King David, whom God set over Israel for ever, had seemed to be destroyed by the broils of history and the ambition of powerful neighbours. Yet here it is named as the root from which God will raise a new king for his people, a king above all other kings of the earth; and, more, this withered stump, this apparently dead tree, is to be a beacon of hope for all who see it. Jesus is the one through whom God can raise up out of all our dead hopes and apparent disasters a salvation that will not just bring us joy, but also be a saving sign to the world around us: God makes all things new.

❖ Father, help me to trust you even if I cannot see your plan for me.
I ask you especially for *[here name your intention]*
Our Father - Hail Mary - Glory Be

Fourth Day: O Clavis David (20th December)

O key of David and sceptre of Israel, what you open no one else can close again; what you close no one can open. O come to lead the captive from prison; free those who sit in darkness and in the shadow of death.

Here, Jesus is named the key that opens all doors, unchains all prisoners and lets light into all dark places. There is no lock or bar or prison-house that can stand against him. We may not be literally in prison, although we might be; but all of us have known, or will some time know, the tomb-like prison of our thoughts, our circumstances, our sins. Jesus Christ can unlock all of these prisons; he can shed light where we are certain no light can ever come. He can lead us into the light, and set us free.

❖ Father, unlock for me all that bars my way; free me from all my imprisonments.
I ask you especially for *[here name your intention]*
Our Father - Hail Mary - Glory Be

Fifth Day: O Oriens (21st December)

O Rising Sun, you are the splendour of eternal light and the sun of justice. O come and enlighten those who sit in darkness and in the shadow of death.

Even in the depths of winter, or perhaps especially then, the breaking light of dawn brings forgotten colours and brilliant light to a world long grey. The morning sun transforms the world. During the long night, we may have become unable to imagine anything except unchanging and unending blackness; but dawn shatters this illusion, and brings light into our eyes and our hearts. So does Jesus Christ work in the long night of our sin and hopelessness.

❖ Father, shed light in my darkness.
I ask you especially for *[here name your intention]*
Our Father - Hail Mary - Glory Be

Sixth Day: O Rex Gentium (22nd December)

O King whom all the peoples desire, you are the cornerstone which makes all one. O come and save man whom you made from clay.

A true king is one who stands as a father to all his people, and is merciful to all; he brings all together, like the cornerstone that binds together a building. Jesus Christ gathers all our hopes and aspirations into his kingdom, and will bring all to fulfilment. We may be clay, weak and malleable; but once fired by his spirit, and together with our neighbours, we can be strong bricks in a mighty building.

❖ Father, strengthen my weakness; have mercy on my hopes. I ask you especially for *[here name your intention]*
Our Father - Hail Mary - Glory Be

Seventh Day: O Emmanuel (23rd December)

O Emmanuel, you are our king and judge, the One whom the peoples await and their Saviour. O come and save us, Lord, our God.

Emmanuel is a Hebrew name that means "God is with us". The birth of Jesus makes this literally true: God has taken on our human condition in all its weakness and its glory, and stands now eternally on our side. All human hopes and aspirations throughout history find their completion in him; all our needs and yearnings are taken up into God's hands, and in Jesus Christ they are transfigured. God is on our side, always.

❖ Father, help me to know you are with me.
I ask you especially for *[here name your intention]*
Our Father - Hail Mary - Glory Be

Eighth Day: Christmas Eve

When the sun rises in the heavens you will see the king of kings. He comes forth from the Father like a bridegroom coming in splendour from his wedding chamber.

Here, the words of Psalm 18 are applied to Christ coming in splendour like the sun at dawn; but the splendour is that of a human child, a baby, weak and apparently helpless. This paradox of strength shown in weakness is one of the core truths of the Christian life: it is when we freely admit our own absolute inability to do what we must do that God is most able to act in us: to lend us the strength, and the love, that we know for certain we cannot find in ourselves.

❖ Father, help me not to be afraid of my weakness; help me to trust in your strength.
I ask you especially for *[here name your intention]*
Our Father - Hail Mary - Glory Be

Ninth Day: Christmas Day

Today Christ is born, today the Saviour has appeared; today the angels sing on earth, the archangels rejoice; today upright men shout out for joy: Glory be to God on high, alleluia.

These words are so familiar to us that we may find them hard to grasp. But all creation, men and women and angels and archangels, and even the watching beasts in the stable or on the hillside, all living things are somehow filled with a joy, a happiness, that wells from the very depths of their being. God has come to make good all that we lack, to repair all that is broken, restore all that is lost, and give us new eyes to see him at work in us and around us, and new hearts to praise him. We may not feel the truth of this, or see what it has got to do with our lives in the here and now. Nevertheless, we live in a world renewed, and its song of joy can be sung by our voices too, if we will let it.

❖ Father, help me to be joyful; help me not to be afraid to be happy.
I ask you especially for *[here name your intention]*
Our Father - Hail Mary - Glory Be

Immaculate Conception (8th December)

The Immaculate Conception is a title given to the Blessed Virgin Mary. We have been freed from sin by Christ but we were conceived and born bearing the sin of Adam - rebellion against God. Mary, however, was redeemed by Christ before she was conceived (God is not constrained by time) and was never separated from God's will. She can teach us how to live in God's will, which we fear may only limit or judge us, but which is in fact perfect freedom.

Many of the authorised apparitions of the Virgin Mary (such as that to St Bernadette at Lourdes) have been under this aspect, of her who is the Immaculate Conception.

To finish this novena on the eve of the feast, you should begin it on 29th November; to finish it on the feast itself, begin on 30th November.

First Day

Mother, sin never separated you from God. I ask you to help me want this union too. May I see that my true happiness lies in the plan God has lovingly created for each of our lives.

❖ I ask you especially for *[here name your intention]*
Our Father - Hail Mary - Glory Be

Second Day

When the Angel announced God's will to you, you accepted it, trusting in God's love. Help me to believe that the Lord wants to do marvels for me.

❖ I ask you especially for *[here name your intention]*
Our Father - Hail Mary - Glory Be

Third Day

You gave birth to the Light of the World. May I be enlightened to see my life as God sees it and not as it is shown to me by Satan, the father of lies.

❖ I ask you especially for *[here name your intention]*
Our Father - Hail Mary - Glory Be

Fourth Day

You are the one who crushes the head of the serpent. Help me to want to crush the evil in my heart. May I call on your help when the devil calls me to sin or despair.

❖ I ask you especially for *[here name your intention]*
Our Father - Hail Mary - Glory Be

Fifth Day

When you appeared to St Catherine Labouré you showed yourself standing on the world and ready to pray for all who ask you. I ask your intercession for all my needs and for the needs of the world.

❖ I ask you especially for *[here name your intention]*
Our Father - Hail Mary - Glory Be

Sixth Day

St Bernadette was not educated or important but you called her to be your messenger. I pray that you help me to announce the love of God in my life, asking him to show me how and where.

❖ I ask you especially for *[here name your intention]*
Our Father - Hail Mary - Glory Be

Seventh Day

At Lourdes you show your concern for the sick and suffering. Help me to enter the sickness and sufferings of my life, believing the Father allows this in love, and help me to offer my sufferings, believing that this can save the world.

❖ I ask you especially for *[here name your intention]*
Our Father - Hail Mary - Glory Be

Eighth Day

St Maximilian Kolbe dedicated his life to you and in this relationship was able literally to offer his life for another. I pray that you help me to offer up my life for my neighbour in whichever way I am asked.

❖ I ask you especially for *[here name your intention]*

Our Father - Hail Mary - Glory Be

Ninth Day

You are the first and perfect disciple. May I imitate you in your love for your Son. Help me to see how to take you as my Mother.

❖ I ask you especially for *[here name your intention]*

Our Father - Hail Mary - Glory Be

Christmas

The feast of Christmas extends over eight days, in what the Church calls an octave. Only the very greatest feasts of the year are like this.

The Christmas octave runs from Christmas Day itself until the 1st January, when we mark the feast of his mother Mary, under her title Mother of God. In between, the Church opens for us the Gospels of the very earliest days of Jesus's life; but it also shows us three feasts of saints whose very different lives were marked with persecution for the sake of Jesus's name. These are not melancholy days, though, for brooding on suffering and opposition; rather, let us recognise how the transforming presence of God in the world and in the lives of human beings brings joy and lightness into the darkest places, and allows forgiveness and mercy to find a home in us, whose nature is often so unforgiving.

First Day: 25th December (Midnight)

Lk 2:1-14

Luke locates Jesus's birth at a precise historical moment (although he may have got some of his dates wrong) and repeatedly stresses that Jesus comes of the royal line of King David. Yet the news comes first not to the great men of Israel, but to shepherds, poor and outside the town on the cold hills. So, whilst it is important to acknowledge that Jesus's coming to us is an historical fact - something that really happened - and that he has all the proper credentials of the promised Messiah, the one whom the people of Israel were expecting to deliver them from their enemies, the central message here is that God comes first to the poor, the neglected, the marginalised, however this poverty and neglect is manifest (and it may not be physical). This remains true today.

❖ Lord, come to me in my poverty; help me to bring you to others.
I ask you especially for *[here name your intention]*
Our Father - Hail Mary - Glory Be

Second Day: 25th December (Dawn)

Lk 2:15-20

The shepherds hurry to the stable to see the sign they have been promised. When they arrive, their news causes astonishment and leaves their hearers bewildered. Babies are born all the time, in all sorts of unlikely places; what is so unusual about this birth that God's own angels are so excited about it? Awe at the revealed glory of God is surely combined with puzzlement. What is all this about? Mary carefully keeps these events in her memory, to reflect on later.

We know this scene so well that it is unlikely to have the same sort of impact on us; we need to imitate Mary, and guard these things in our hearts. A saviour has come into the world, as a human child; what does this mean for me? From what oppression do I need to be set free? Do I trust that God will keep his promises, and fulfil the signs he has given me (if I have even recognised them)?

❖ Lord, help me to see my need of you; help me to welcome your coming into my life, and to bring this news to others.

I ask you especially for *[here name your intention]*

Our Father - Hail Mary - Glory Be

Third Day: 26th December (St Stephen)
Mt 10:17-22

It seems strange, perhaps, that the day after Christmas is dedicated to the first Christian martyr, St Stephen, stoned to death for witnessing to Jesus. This reminds us, maybe, that one of the possible reactions to the baffling arrival of the Messiah amongst us is fear, uncomprehending opposition, and even anger and violence. We may feel these reactions ourselves; we should certainly, the Gospel warns us, expect to meet them in others. But we need not worry about this. God's Spirit will be with us in our need, and will lend us the words and strength we need. St Stephen prayed for those who killed him, but also knew they did not know what they were doing.

❖ Lord, help me not to fear you, and not to let my fear become anger; help me to forgive, and be forgiven.
I ask you especially for *[here name your intention]*
Our Father - Hail Mary - Glory Be

Fourth Day: 27th December (St John the Evangelist)
Jn 20:2-8

Now we are somewhere different again: the empty tomb on Easter morning. The Church today celebrates the feast of the Apostle John, author of the Gospel, and traditionally identified with the unnamed "beloved disciple" of this passage. The paramount witness of his life, this Gospel suggests, is this moment, when he first knows that God has passed through death and destroyed it. This is the ultimate end and purpose of the birth of Jesus; this baby will become the one who is tortured and dies for his people - who by his own suffering transforms all the pain and death of the world. No longer is it meaningless, but a way for the world to be saved.

❖ Lord, be with me in all I experience; help me to know you have defeated death and pain.

I ask you especially for *[here name your intention]*
Our Father - Hail Mary - Glory Be

Fifth Day: 28th December (Holy Innocents)
Mt 2:13-18

Even closer to the birth of Jesus is the brutal massacre of the male children of Bethlehem (whom the Church calls the Holy Innocents). There is a peculiar horror and shock produced by the deliberate killing of a child. How can God allow such things? In our day, the horror of abortion, which has destroyed millions of unborn lives, probably evokes similar bafflement (if we consider it at all. Most people do not.).

But perhaps we should ask ourselves, instead, not why God allows such things, but why human beings permit them. This Gospel also shows us St Joseph acting to save Mary and Jesus from Herod; and the Church, in remembering these nameless children as holy, assures us that God has them in his hand. We should look, first, to our own hearts.

❖ Lord, help me to protect the innocent.
I ask you especially for *[here name your intention]*
Our Father - Hail Mary - Glory Be

Sixth Day: 29th December

Lk 2:22-35

From his earliest days, Jesus is enfolded by the customs and observances of the Mosaic Law. He is taken to the Temple, the heart of Jerusalem, the holy city. There he is to be presented to the Lord, as the Law decrees every firstborn male child must be. And there again, as in Bethlehem, Mary and Joseph are confronted with a baffling event: an old man comes over and claims their child is the one God has sent to save Israel, and overturn the settled order of things. Making this announcement crowns his life's work. In one sense, we too are called as Christians to be like Simeon, to announce Jesus to others, and leave the rest to God. But this happens in God's time, and not ours.

❖ Lord, teach me to be patient, to wait for you; and help me to recognise you when you appear, in however unexpected a guise.

I ask you especially for *[here name your intention]*

Our Father - Hail Mary - Glory Be

Seventh Day: 30th December

Lk 2:36-40

We can easily overlook or make fun of pious old ladies, who like Anna daughter of Phanuel seem to be constantly in church, praying for something or other, lighting candles, running mysterious errands in the sacristy. Even when they are not actively mad (and many of them are), they can be a nuisance or a distraction. Yet whatever their faults or foibles, their short temper or uncertain personal hygiene, they give an undeniable and constant witness of prayer. We would do well, perhaps, to imitate more than we judge.

❖ Lord, help me to see others as you see them.
I ask you especially for *[here name your intention]*
Our Father - Hail Mary - Glory Be

Eighth Day: 31st December

Jn 1:1-18

After the various circumstantial details of Jesus's birth, and the events of his first months, the Church's camera tracks back and gives us a look at the big picture. The Prologue to John's Gospel can seem like a forbidding and rather opaque philosophical tract, but at its heart is a simple assertion: the Word was made flesh, and dwelt amongst us. God has lived amongst his people, and all we know and are, he has known too and been. Nothing now need daunt or frighten us; the primordial light, the pattern and energy of all things, him through whom all came to be: this Word of God we know as Jesus, born as a human baby, just as we were.

❖ Lord, help me to know your glory.
I ask you especially for *[here name your intention]*
Our Father - Hail Mary - Glory Be

Ninth Day: 1st January (Mary, Mother of God)

Lk 2:16-21

On this last day of the octave, which is also the first day of the calendar year, we return to where we began, with the shepherds visiting the stable. There is, however, one small but important addition: the child is now named: Jesus, which means "God saves". In the Judaism of this time, only the father names a son: so by naming Jesus as part of the rite of circumcision, Joseph adopts him into the line and house of David. But they are poor: when Jesus is presented at the Temple, Joseph and Mary bring only the poor man's offering of two doves. Mary is not now named the mother of a king, but Mother of God.

We, like Mary, should gather in our hearts what we have seen and experienced, and we will see, perhaps, that much looks the same as before; but now, at the centre of the picture, is the man Jesus.

❖ Lord, let me in my weakness know your saving power. I ask you especially for *[here name your intention]*

Our Father - Hail Mary - Glory Be

Epiphany

The Gospels of the days of Christmastide are a sort of overture to the public ministry of Jesus. They fall into two halves, either side of the feast of Epiphany. That feast, which means "The Revealing" or "The Making Known" is the point at which Jesus's birth, which has already been announced to the Jewish people in the person of the shepherds, is now made known to the rest of the world. The wise men, however, have already got an inkling of the event; indeed, they are rather better informed than Herod and his learned advisers. This reminds us not to scorn the wisdom and insight of those apparently outside the Church; God has ways to make himself known to them too.

Before the Epiphany, John the Baptist announces that Jesus is coming; after the Epiphany, we have a sort of whirlwind summary of Jesus's preaching and healing.

The feast of the Epiphany is the first sign that Jesus's mission is not just to the people of Israel, the bearers of the promise, but also to all the children of Adam and Eve. This remains true. God's love and mercy extend to all people, no matter how far away they may seem - whether physically, in those parts of the world remotest from where the Church has historically flourished, or in terms of their way of life. Jesus Christ came to call sinners, and associated with outcasts and the morally compromised: prostitutes, tax-collectors (who were the hated collaborators of an occupying power), lepers. No one is outside God's mercy; however far we may feel ourselves from "proper Christian behaviour" in whatever way, God remains close to us. He shows himself to us in his vulnerability; we in our turn should feel able to share with him our deepest fears and anxieties, our failures and shame, our concern for those we know who seem to live as if nothing matters very much. These are exactly the situations where Jesus is most present.

First Day (2nd January)

Jn 1:19-25 (A voice crying in the wilderness)

The religious authorities in Jerusalem do not understand who this man, John the Baptist, is, nor why he is acting as he does. Immersing in the river people who came to him, in answer to his call to repent, to mark a change in their lives and their undertaking to live again by God's Law, was a powerful sign associated with the Messiah, the king whom Jewish tradition expected to come and rescue his people from oppression and sin. Was John claiming to be the Messiah? He was not; he was, he declared, merely a forerunner, a sign of the one whom God was about to send.

We may have similar questions for the Church. What is the point of it all? What is the purpose of the sacraments we are invited to, especially confession and the Eucharist? These are not done primarily for the sake of the Church, to gain it status or our dutiful obedience, or the reflected glory of pomp and ceremonial, although sometimes people within the Church act as if this were so. No: the Church's aim in all this is to make us ready to receive Jesus - to prepare our hearts for the arrival of God. All of our questions are best answered by the person of Jesus, the Christ: the Messiah.

❖ Father, help me to make a path for Jesus to come to me. I ask you especially for *[here name your intention]*

Our Father - Hail Mary - Glory Be

Second Day (3rd January)

Jn 1:29-34 (Behold the Lamb of God)

When John sees Jesus, he recognises him as the One he has been announcing, even though he did not know him by sight (Luke's Gospel makes the two cousins, but we may suppose they had not seen one another much since early childhood). He is the one who will baptise with the Holy Spirit - that is, who can produce a real change of heart in us. When we meet him, we will know him, because the Holy Spirit is with him. The undying life, the joy that is not destroyed by the great or small deaths we encounter each day, this is the Spirit in us. When we meet this, we will know that Jesus is there.

❖ Father, send me your Spirit, so I may know Jesus.
I ask you especially for *[here name your intention]*

Our Father - Hail Mary - Glory Be

Third Day (4th January)

Jn 1:35-42 (We have found the Messiah)

Again, John points Jesus out to others. This time, two of them, hitherto his own disciples, follow Jesus, and make a formal request to become his disciples instead (this is the meaning of their question, "Rabbi, where do you live?"). In turn, one of them tells his brother "we have found the Messiah", and this brother, Simon, is given a new name - which means, in scriptural terms, a new identity in God's eyes. When we are brought to Jesus, he gives us a new identity, too: this is most obviously symbolised in the new name we are given in baptism, but at a deep level means that only by meeting Jesus can we come to know our true selves, who we really are in God's eyes, rather than the various masks and roles we sedulously assume for our own purposes. Only by living in this our true self can we be happy.

❖ Father, tell me my true name; help me to be my true self, as you alone know me.
I ask you especially for *[here name your intention]*

Our Father - Hail Mary - Glory Be

Fourth Day (5th January)

Jn 1:43-51 (You are the Son of God, you are the King of Israel)

This is a strange and slightly puzzling passage. Why is Nathanael so amazed that Jesus saw him under a fig tree? And why does this mean Jesus knows he is a righteous man, "incapable of deceit", a model Israelite? We have a sense that more is going on than we are ever likely to understand. But whatever the undisclosed meanings here, they lead Nathanael, like Philip before him, to recognise Jesus as the Messiah, the one who is sent by God to free them and rule over them in God's name. Jesus tells him then that he will see angels going up and down from him to heaven. This is an echo of the dream that came to Jacob, who became Israel, the father of the Twelve Tribes, as recorded in Genesis 28. Jesus is claiming to be the new Israel, the renewer of God's holy people.

The signs by which God speaks to us may be opaque or trivial-looking to others; but they are the exact way God has for talking to our hearts, and we should not despise them because they do not look like what we expected. Jesus comes to make all things new; to renew in us the promise of God.

❖ Father, help me to listen when you speak to me.
I ask you especially for *[here name your intention]*
Our Father - Hail Mary - Glory Be

Fifth Day (6th January: the Epiphany)

Mt 2:1-12 (The wise men come to pay homage)

In Jesus's time, as in ours, the mysterious East was the expected home of inscrutable but often accurate spiritual insight. God's message announcing freedom for humanity has come a good deal more clearly to the Magi (magician-astronomers, if you like, who practised their art in the service of religion) than to the professional experts of Herod's court, or the Jerusalem Temple. This may well be in part because the substance of the message (that salvation will come in the shape of a child born in an obscure small town, far from the centres of influence and learning) is so unexpected, and on the face of it frankly ridiculous. How can this event make any sort of difference to us? Yet the Magi, in a matter-of-fact way, walk easily in this dream-like world of visions and celestial signs, and give their gifts, precious and symbolic, before vanishing as silently as they appeared. In their wake, the politico-religious establishment is profoundly disturbed, even though all the child has done so far is be born.

God is not constrained by what we expect, or disturbed by our panicked reactions to his appearance in our lives. Let us try to welcome him, and offer him what we have, rather than trying to second-guess what he is about before we will give him house-room.

❖ Father, help me to find Jesus and not be afraid.
I ask you especially for *[here name your intention]*
Our Father - Hail Mary - Glory Be

Sixth Day (7th January)

Mt 4:12-17, 23-25 (John is arrested; Jesus begins to preach)

Only when John is arrested does Jesus begin to preach. His message is identical to John's: repent, because God's kingdom is very near. But Jesus, unlike John, accompanies words by signs: he heals those who are sick or afflicted; nor does he stay in one place and allow people to come to him, as John did. Instead, he goes throughout Galilee, to those who dwell in shadow and darkness, and seeks out those who are lost, to bring them light and healing.

God does not expect us to do everything, or indeed very much. He comes to find us wherever we are, however dark or obscure the place we find ourselves in. All he asks is that we turn to him when we hear his voice.

❖ Father, help me to hear you and turn to you.
I ask you especially for *[here name your intention]*
Our Father - Hail Mary - Glory Be

Seventh Day (8th January)

Mk 6:34-44 (The feeding of the five thousand)

The crowds who come to find Jesus are lost and helpless, like a mob of sheep; they have come after him without bothering to think about obvious things like food or shelter, or what time it is. His disciples, too, are also pretty hopeless: their main goal is to be reassured that this is someone else's problem, and nothing they need be worried about. Jesus does not let them off the hook; but he at the same time provides all that they need to do what he asks them, in a way that goes beyond anything they could have expected.

We very often try to find reasons not to do anything to help, to avoid a situation that God presents us with. We can't possibly do anything, we reckon, so it must be someone else's problem, not ours. Jesus does not work like this. He tells the disciples what to do, and then gives them what they need to do it.

❖ Father, help me not to look for excuses but instead to trust you will provide what I need.

I ask you especially for *[here name your intention]*

Our Father - Hail Mary - Glory Be

Eighth Day (9th January)

Mk 6:45-52 (Jesus walks on the lake - do not be afraid)

Now the disciples are trying to cross a lake at evening, against a headwind, after Jesus has insisted they make the crossing. He comes past them, walking on the waves, but stops to help them only when in their fear and distress they call out to him. Then the wind drops, and their fear is replaced by utter bewilderment. What on earth is going on? Who is this? Feeding five thousand men and uncounted women and children with five loaves has clearly not made any lasting impression on them.

Like the disciples, sometimes we find ourselves out on a limb - in the middle of a metaphorical (or perhaps an actual) lake, in a high wind, far from shore, after doing something that Jesus has appeared to tell us to do. The sight of him passing by at a distance, defying what we reckon are the settled laws of existence, is no obvious comfort to us; in fact, it may make our distress only deeper. Like the disciples, at these moments we must call out to him; and he will come to us. Unlike the disciples, we must remember what he has already done in our lives. He will not abandon us now.

❖ Father, help me to call to you in my distress; help me to remember your mighty works.

I ask you especially for *[here name your intention]*

Our Father - Hail Mary - Glory Be

Ninth Day (10th January)

Lk 4:14-22 (This text is being fulfilled today even as you listen)

Now Jesus returns to his home town, and goes to the synagogue. There he reads a passage from Isaiah that more or less openly declares he is the promised Messiah: "the Lord has anointed me…This text is being fulfilled today even as you listen". But it is the details of his mission that are important. He is not a triumphant king, driving the Roman oppressor out of the Holy Land and restoring the Kingdom of Israel to the glory it had under David and Solomon; he brings sight to the blind, freedom to the imprisoned, good news to the poor and downtrodden. A good king might do some of these things; but only after his enemies were overthrown and his rule re-established. Jesus promises these things first; and from this beginning, God's kingdom will grow. It is not limited by the covenant with Israel, but is open to the whole world.

We need Jesus to open our eyes, free us from imprisonment, bring joy to our poor and downtrodden hearts; then we, too, may help bring these things to others. Jesus's example suggests another profound truth: it is by bringing these things (light, freedom, consolation) to others first, not to ourselves, that our own hurts may be healed.

❖ Father, help me to hear your good news, and to bring it to others.

I ask you especially for *[here name your intention]*

Our Father - Hail Mary - Glory Be

Annunciation (25th March)

For much of Christian history, this feast - celebrated on 25th March, nine months before Christmas - marked the beginning of the year. This may seem odd at first sight, and our modern adoption of 1st January much more obvious and straightforward, but there is a profound truth here: the Annunciation, the visit of the angel Gabriel to the young girl, Mary of Nazareth, and her response to his offer from God, is the very turning-point of human history. At this moment, when Mary says "yes" to God, the Incarnation - God's life with us, as one of us - begins, in the womb of a virgin. From this moment, everything is different. God is amongst us; God is on our side. Just as Jesus grew slowly in the months before his human birth, so he grows in us - God's gift of undying life - slowly, once we accept his word into our hearts.

Every time we say the *Hail Mary*, we remember, and make present, the message of God to Mary, given through the angel; and we ask that this come to pass in us, too, in God's time and with the watchful prayers of the Virgin to help us.

To finish this novena on the eve of the feast, you should begin it on 16th March; to finish on the feast itself, begin on 17th March.

First Day: Hail

No one addresses anyone today using the greeting "Hail!", except humorously or in badly-scripted historical drama ("Hail Caesar! The Armies of the North salute you!" and so on). But originally it was a quite normal greeting; it is from the Old English *wes thu hael*, "may you be well". Here it translates a Greek word, χαιρε, which is the corresponding normal greeting amongst speakers of New Testament Greek, and means "rejoice, be glad". Both the English and the Greek words share a basic sense of wishing for another person wholeness and fulness of life: health and happiness, broadly understood, are two ways of expressing the same thing. "May you be the person God knows you to be" is a cumbersome way of expressing this, but might be the best way to look at the ultimate implications of these greetings. For Mary, the fulness of life lies in accepting the role God has chosen her for, as mother of his Son; for us, too, true life is in saying yes to God and his plans for us, however unlikely or plain ridiculous these may seem.

❖ Father, help me to accept the fulness of life.
I ask you especially for *[here name your intention]*
Our Father - Hail Mary - Glory Be

Second Day: Mary

The name Mary is our form of the Aramaic name *Maryam*, which derives from the Hebrew *Miriam*. Its Latin and Greek form is *Maria*. The meaning of the name is obscure; it may be related to an Egyptian root *mr*, "love", or *myr*, "beloved", but other etymologies have been suggested.

The first Miriam found in Scripture is the elder sister of Moses, who hid him in the bulrushes where he was found by Pharaoh's daughter; she also suggested Moses's mother as a nurse for the infant. Later, Miriam sings the song of triumph over Pharaoh's army drowned in the Red Sea, a song we still sing each year at the Easter Vigil (see *Ex* 15:20-21). Mary, mother of Jesus, echoes these later roles: she takes the child Jesus into safety in Egypt from Herod; she sings her *Magnificat* celebrating God's triumph through the poor and unregarded.

❖ Father, help me to know Mary as my mother.
I ask you especially for *[here name your intention]*
Our Father - Hail Mary - Glory Be

Third Day: full

The next three words in English, "full of grace", are two words in Latin (*gratia plena*) and in Greek, only a single word: κεχαριτωμένη. This has been sometimes translated "highly favoured" (which, in at least one well-known Christmas carol, has become "highly-flavoured (gravy)" to generations of schoolboys) but "full of grace" brings out the sense well enough.

Full: empty of self-will and her own plans, Mary is able to be filled by God. His life takes root in her to such an extent that, uniquely, she becomes physically fruitful: God comes forth from her in the person of the child Jesus. We, too, are called to be filled with God, although in our case the birth this presages is that of God's life in us - the life of undying love, of love that death cannot conquer, of life that death cannot quench. We too are to bring Christ to the world, but not as a physically separate person like Mary's son, the child Jesus, but through the medium of our own minds and bodies, our own joys and sorrows and kindnesses, that allow us to be in a strong sense Christ for those around us.

❖ Father, let Jesus be born in me.
I ask you especially for *[here name your intention]*

Our Father - Hail Mary - Glory Be

Fourth Day: of

This is a small and usually overlooked word, but it is charged with mystery. If one thing is "of" another, it is somehow enfolded in it, it belongs to it, it issues from it, and yet it has its own separate being. Things both belong to each other, are included in each other, and are yet distinct one from another. We are both one and many. This may sound hopelessly vague and "mystical", but in fact we are all of us, even those who think of ourselves as ruthlessly pragmatic and practical, effortlessly comfortable with this concept, since we have been unconsciously deploying it, since childhood, whenever we say "of". This relationship, encompassing both inclusion and separateness, may stand as a type, a pattern, of our relationship with God. We are "of" God; God is "of" us.

❖ Father, help me to know that you are with me.
I ask you especially for *[here name your intention]*
Our Father - Hail Mary - Glory Be

Fifth Day: grace

Theologians have made much of the concept of grace, analysing it into various technical categories (created and uncreated, prevenient, habitual and actual, sufficient and efficacious) that most will find either baffling or pernickety. In sum, though, grace means the action or presence of God in the Christian life. Some writers talk about "graces", meaning by that a particular manifestation of God's presence or action in the experience of the Christian. In both senses, Mary is full of grace: God is present and acts through her, and she witnesses God's action and presence in all she experiences. We are called to be like her, who "stored up all these things in her heart" (*Lk* 2:51).

❖ Father, help me to be alive to your presence in my life.
I ask you especially for *[here name your intention]*
Our Father - Hail Mary - Glory Be

Sixth Day: the Lord

The Jewish people reckoned the name of God, as told to Moses, too holy to be spoken aloud; only once a year, in the Holy of Holies in the Temple on the Day of Atonement (Yom Kippur), might the High Priest utter this name. When reading any passage of Scripture in which this name (the Holy Tetragrammaton, the four letters) appears, one says instead another title of God, most usually *Adonai*, "the Lord". Adonai, which in Greek is rendered *kyrios*, is the one to whom all things belong, for whom all things are made, to whose ends all things work, knowingly or not. God is Lord of all things: everything we are, have, experience or witness, all these things belong to him, and reveal his hand to the eye and heart willing to see it; and all things ultimately do his will, whether they know it or not.

❖ Father, let me welcome you as Lord of my life.
I ask you especially for *[here name your intention]*
Our Father - Hail Mary - Glory Be

Seventh Day: is

This is another small word of immense importance. Gabriel declares to Mary that "the Lord *is* with thee": "is" signifies that the presence of God is not something in our memory (although we should remember his mighty deeds with us and throughout salvation history) or in some wished-for future, but something that happens now, at the very moment

I am writing this sentence, or you are reading it. In all the events, great or small, of our daily lives, God is there; God sends us all these things to touch our hearts through them, if only we are willing to see it. God's time is always now. By saying the Lord "is" with her, the angel declares that God is present and acting at that very moment. He joins together two things, God and the Virgin Mary, by naming them and joining those names with "is". Words, we should remember, are potent things; we should not use them lightly.

❖ Father, help me to be present in this moment, which is your moment.
I ask you especially for *[here name your intention]*
Our Father - Hail Mary - Glory Be

Eighth Day: with

God is "with" Mary: he is both intimately present to her, as he is to us all, but in her case, with the added dimension of the physical presence of Jesus in her womb, and also "with" her in the related sense that he is on her side: God stands "with" her in all the events of her life, and lends her his strength and love. So it is for us: God is with us, in our hearts and in all the people and events we meet; but he is also with us, on our side, a strong helper in distress and the one who rejoices in our happiness. God is not neutral or indifferent; he is our passionate advocate and defender, and the merciful father who welcomes us home.

❖ Father, be with me all the days of my life.
I ask you especially for *[here name your intention]*
Our Father - Hail Mary - Glory Be

Ninth Day: thee

We may imagine the old second person pronouns "thee" and "thou" are somehow ceremonious or formal, and belong to high etiquette and stilted courtesy. In fact almost the opposite is true. These were intimate forms, words used between parent and child, husband and wife, brother and sister. In many languages even today, asking someone to address you by the less formal pronoun (for which the French, for example, even have a particular word: *tutoyer*) is a strong gesture of friendship. So when the angel calls Mary "thee" rather than "you", he is showing her and us that God is as close to us as a mother or father is, as a sibling, as a beloved friend. This is not an archaism preserved out of unthinking reverence for what is old and accustomed, but a sign of God's loving closeness to Mary, and to each of us.

❖ Father, help me to know you love me.
I ask you especially for *[here name your intention]*
Our Father - Hail Mary - Glory Be

Easter

Easter is the centre of the whole Christian year, the point around which all the Church's worship and belief  turns. To bring out the riches of this feast, it is extended into an "octave", that is, the following week, which together with Easter Sunday itself makes eight days, a number that to the ancients signified completion or fulfilment. During these days, the Gospels at Mass present the various appearances of the risen Jesus after his Resurrection, and show the ways he transforms the lives of his disciples, who (unsurprisingly) were confused and distraught after his crucifixion and death. Jesus, risen from the dead, comes to them and renews them; he grants them a share in his new life, the life of Easter, life that has passed through death and destroyed it. This life, eternal life, he offers to us too, not merely in some abstract future state, but here and now, as we are, in all our defeats and confusions. During this octave, we can place ourselves within these Gospels, and allow Jesus to come to us, as he came to his first disciples.

The last day of the Easter Octave, known as the Second Sunday of Easter, was named by St John Paul II as the

Sunday of the Divine Mercy. We are invited to make our own the doubts and fears of the disciples, and offer them to God our Father, who is rich in mercy, and who, through Jesus, sends us the Spirit that allows us to know ourselves forgiven, and in our turn to have mercy on others.

First Day: the Easter Vigil

Mt 28:1-10; *Mk* 16:1-7; *Lk* 24:1-12 (The women go to the tomb)

It is dawn, the day after the sabbath, and the women who followed Jesus are on their way to the tomb. They are coming as early as they can without breaking God's Law of sabbath rest. The angel tells them "Do not be afraid. He is not here, he is risen". Then, when they meet Jesus himself, he repeats the message: "Do not be afraid".

❖ Father, often I put off or delay what I need to do; help me to have the same zeal as these disciples, and not to be mastered by my fears.
I ask you especially for *[here name your intention]*
Our Father - Hail Mary - Glory Be

Second Day: Easter Day

Jn 20:1-9 (Peter and John run to the tomb)

When they hear the baffling news that Jesus's body has disappeared, Peter and John run to see for themselves. There is a strong emphasis on the factual nature of their witness: first one looks in, then the other goes in, and they see specific cloths in particular places. The Church has always insisted on the physical fact of the Resurrection; but also on its mysterious nature. The life that Jesus passes to, the life we are offered, is rich and strange, but rooted in the same physical world we know.

❖ Father, help me not to be slow to follow the truth; help me to live the life you promise.
I ask you especially for *[here name your intention]*
Our Father - Hail Mary - Glory Be

Third Day: Easter Monday

Mt 28:8-15 (Jesus meets the women in the garden)

After meeting the angel, the women set off to tell the others. Almost at once, they run into Jesus himself. He gives them another message for the disciples. Meanwhile, the chief priests and soldiers come up with a cover story about a stolen body: "to this day that is the story among the Jews".

We can be very ready to explain away the apparently clear action of God in our lives. Human beings are very good at refusing to see the big picture. We should not be credulous or gullible, or see extraordinary miracles everywhere: God generally works through "ordinary" things (what the philosophers call "secondary causes"). But we should not dismiss events lightly; God is at work in exactly the small and overlooked things; the day-to-day action of our lives is charged with his presence, if only we have eyes to see it.

❖ Father, help me to see your work.
I ask you especially for *[here name your intention]*
Our Father - Hail Mary - Glory Be

Fourth Day: Easter Tuesday

Jn 20:11-18 (Mary of Magdala meets Jesus)

In the story given in John's Gospel, whilst Peter and John are running back with their shocking news, Mary of Magdala is still hanging about the garden. She despairs of finding Jesus's body; and when she meets him "she did not recognise him". Only when he calls her by name does she know him. Then she seems to want to take physical hold of him, which he gently discourages. Perhaps we should see here that what is most important is not the precise physical character of the Resurrection, but the way in which we find ourselves truly only when named by God. Only God knows us; only he can help us to know ourselves, and thus be ourselves, and be capable of true joy and true sorrow.

❖ Father, help me to meet you and recognise you.
I ask you especially for *[here name your intention]*
Our Father - Hail Mary - Glory Be

Fifth Day: Easter Wednesday

Lk 24:13-35 (the road to Emmaus)

We don't know exactly where Emmaus is, but we do know that when the disciples were on their way there, they were going the wrong way. Jesus falls into step with them, and eventually turns them around. He turns them, in fact, both in the literal sense that they retrace their steps back to Jerusalem, and in the metaphorical sense that he takes their depression, their frustration and disappointment, and turns them into joy and zeal. Their encounter culminates, and Jesus is revealed, when he breaks bread with them. Until this moment, the fact that they had already heard the news about the Resurrection had made no difference to them.

If I have taken a wrong turning, Jesus comes to me in the Scriptures, in the Eucharist, in a chance encounter with an apparent stranger, to set me on the right path again. No amount of factual knowledge of itself will do this: only meeting the Risen Lord.

❖ Father, help me to see things as they truly are, not as they suit my own narrative, especially if that is one of despair or self-pity.

I ask you especially for *[here name your intention]*

Our Father - Hail Mary - Glory Be

Sixth Day: Easter Thursday

Lk 24:35-48 (Jesus is not a ghost)

This Gospel follows immediately on from the previous one. The news from the road to Emmaus is corroborated by the news from Jerusalem itself: Jesus has appeared to Peter. But none of this prevents a similar collapse of nerve when Jesus himself comes amongst them all. He has to take strong steps to prove he is really there. Touch me, he says; watch me eat. Jesus is not a ghost. He opens the Scriptures to them: all that has happened is set out there; and also what must happen now. The call to repent and be forgiven must be brought to the whole world, beginning right there, where they are, in Jerusalem.

Sometimes, even after repeated evidence, we cannot believe in a God who loves us and takes an interest in what we do; who wants to save us from our sins and mistakes and fears. Jesus shows us here that God is patient; that if we open the Scriptures, he will speak to us there. And he also tells us that the good news of forgiveness needs to be heard, first of all, where we ourselves are.

❖ Father, help me to know forgiveness; help my disbelief. I ask you especially for *[here name your intention]*
Our Father - Hail Mary - Glory Be

Seventh Day: Easter Friday

Jn 21:1-14 (The disciples go fishing on the Sea of Tiberias)

This story is tacked on to the end of John's Gospel in a sort of appendix. It shows us, again, how hard it is for Jesus's disciples to stay persuaded of anything. After all the excitement of the garden, Emmaus and the Upper Room, Simon Peter and the rest have gone back to their old life on the seashore. They spend a fruitless night fishing, probably because they can think of nothing else to do. Then a stranger calls out instructions, they make a huge catch, and realise it must be Jesus. He cooks them breakfast.

We see, again, how easily we can slip back into our old ways, our old habits and niggles and sins. But we see, also, how Jesus comes to find us, and makes himself known in the most apparently ordinary events. The turning-point of the Gospel passage is the disciple's cry, "It is the Lord!" After that, the whole encounter is charged with meaning (breakfast is more than just breakfast).

❖ Father, help me not to lose heart; come to find me when I lose my way.
I ask you especially for *[here name your intention]*
Our Father - Hail Mary - Glory Be

Eighth Day: Easter Saturday

Mk 16:9-15 (a summary of Jesus's appearances)

This passage is thought by most scholars to be something added to Mark's Gospel at some point after it was first written. This doesn't make it any less a text through which God speaks to us. It gives a brisk and telling summary of Jesus's appearances and his disciples' reactions. First, they didn't believe Mary Magdalene; then they didn't believe the disciples coming back from Emmaus. So Jesus appears to them all in person. He tells them off for being so pig-headed and distrusting. Then he tells them to "proclaim the Good News to all creation".

❖ Like the disciples, I sometimes refuse to believe, and discount others' testimony. Father, be patient with my obstinacy; help me to hear the Good News, and share it with others.

I ask you especially for *[here name your intention]*

Our Father - Hail Mary - Glory Be

Ninth Day: Sunday of the Divine Mercy

Jn 20:19-31 (Jesus gives them the Holy Spirit. Doubting Thomas)

We end, on Divine Mercy Sunday, with another example of God's patience. Jesus first dispels the fears and doubts of the assembled disciples; then he comes back a week later, on the octave day of his Resurrection, to do the same for Thomas, who is sulking and sceptical.

First, Jesus gives his disciples his own spirit, the Spirit that allows us to love and forgive where we know for a certain fact no forgiveness or love is possible. God, the merciful Father, loves us and forgives us in this way, no matter what we have done or how little we think of ourselves. In God's eyes, we are, all of us, beyond price. He loves us, who feel ourselves unlovable, so we may love others. Like Thomas, we can refuse to believe this on the testimony of others; God will give us proof, if we have the courage to ask for it: and that means, perhaps, acting as if we can do what we know we cannot.

❖ Father, help me to know myself loved and forgiven; help me to love and forgive others, as you have loved me.
I ask you especially for *[here name your intention]*
Our Father - Hail Mary - Glory Be

Pentecost

Pentecost, the Feast of Weeks, marks the fiftieth day after Passover in the Jewish calendar (a week of weeks is forty-nine days, plus one for the feast itself). The Church celebrates on this day the descent of the Holy Spirit on the disciples, locked by their fears into the virtual prison of the Upper Room, but suddenly given the same zeal and fire as came down on the Elders of Israel when Moses received the Law on the Holy Mountain, which the Jewish Pentecost or Shavuot called to mind. The Church, it is often said, was born on the day of Pentecost; but it is also a day that reminds us strongly of our enduring ties with the People of the Covenant.

To finish on the feast, begin the novena on the Saturday of the Sixth Week of Easter; to finish on the eve of the feast, begin on the Friday of the Sixth Week.

First Day

Acts 1:9

Although the disciples had lived with Christ and seen his Resurrection and Ascension with their own eyes, their lives had not yet changed. Help me not to live as if faith were only a Sunday obligation, but to see what you have done in my life.

❖ I ask you especially for *[here name your intention]*

Our Father - Hail Mary - Glory Be

Second Day

Acts 1:14

The disciples were with Mary and were praying constantly. I ask you to give me this grace of prayer. I ask you for hope and for the consolation of the love of the Blessed Virgin Mary.

❖ I ask you especially for *[here name your intention]*

Our Father - Hail Mary - Glory Be

Third Day

Acts 1:21-26

After referring to the Scriptures, the disciples chose a replacement for Judas. Matthias joined the Apostles later than the original Twelve, but was not less than the others. Help me to see that no matter how late I come to you, you are waiting for me.

❖ I ask you especially for *[here name your intention]*

Our Father - Hail Mary - Glory Be

Fourth Day

Acts 1:24

Before deciding who should take Judas's place, the disciples prayed together to understand your will. Help me to remember I am not alone; that you are there to help me make decisions and know your will for me. Give me gratitude for the Church where we gather to pray together.

❖ I ask you especially for *[here name your intention]*

Our Father - Hail Mary - Glory Be

Fifth Day

Acts 2:1

The disciples had come together to celebrate the Jewish feast of Shavuot. This feast marks the giving of the Ten Commandments and is on the fiftieth day after Passover, which recalls the freeing of the slaves from Egypt, just as the Christian Pentecost marks fifty days from the Resurrection that breaks our slavery to sin and death. Jewish tradition speaks of the Spirit of God coming down like fire on the seventy elders who accompanied Moses to Mount Sinai (see *Ex* 18-19); they were symbols of the whole human race, which was reckoned to be made up of seventy nations. The account in Acts renews this encounter as the Spirit comes down like fire on the disciples, who then go out and preach in all the languages of the known world.

You always help us to understand new things by using what we already know. Help me to trust that.

❖ I ask you especially for *[here name your intention]*
Our Father - Hail Mary - Glory Be

Sixth Day

Acts 2:2-4

The disciples' lives changed in a moment when they were filled with the Spirit which pushed them to share the gospel. Help me to recognise the impulses that come from you and not to be afraid of what people think of me.

❖ I ask you especially for *[here name your intention]*
Our Father - Hail Mary - Glory Be

Seventh Day

Acts 2:5

Shavuot was a pilgrim festival and people had come to Jerusalem from many other places to celebrate the feast. Help me to know that you never forget any details; that everything that happens does so at the appointed time. Give me the grace to trust in your love.

❖ I ask you especially for *[here name your intention]*
Our Father - Hail Mary - Glory Be

Eighth Day

Acts 2:6-12

When the disciples spoke, each person heard the word in their own language. You know me better than I know myself and you speak to me in my own language. Help me to do the same with others. Help me to speak to them in ways they can understand; help me to accept putting their needs before my own.

❖ I ask you especially for *[here name your intention]*
Our Father - Hail Mary - Glory Be

Ninth Day

Acts 2:14

Peter took the place Christ had prepared for him. The Church was built on him as the Lord had intended. I ask you for love for your Church. Give me the grace to pray with and for the Holy Father, the Pope.

❖ I ask you especially for *[here name your intention]*
Our Father - Hail Mary - Glory Be

Sacred Heart

The modern feast of the Sacred Heart of Jesus derives mainly from a series of visions experienced by a French

nun, St Margaret Mary Alacocque, in the latter part of the seventeenth century. Her visions included a series of twelve "promises" made concerning the graces that would be given to those who practised devotion to Jesus under this aspect. Her near contemporary, the French priest St John Eudes, also wrote much on this devotion.

The feast of the Sacred Heart is celebrated on the Friday after the second Sunday after Pentecost (the first Sunday after Pentecost is always Trinity Sunday; the second, in many places including England & Wales, is the feast of Corpus Christi). This means a novena, to end on the feast itself, should begin on the Thursday after Trinity Sunday; or to end on the eve of the feast, the Wednesday after Trinity Sunday.

St John Eudes taught that Jesus is at the centre of everything and his love, his heart, holds us all. He also saw how much Jesus's mother's love helps us. He wrote: "So closely are Jesus and Mary bound up with each other that whoever beholds Jesus sees Mary; whoever loves Jesus, loves Mary; whoever has devotion to Jesus, has devotion to Mary."

Lord, may I come to know your love for me and also the help of your Blessed Mother in all the difficulties of my life. Help me to know how to live a life devoted to you and to find the peace only you can give.

First Day

St Margaret Mary's visions of you brought her great suffering. Her sisters and superiors were saddened and exasperated by her. Doctors found her silly and attention-seeking. One even told her that if she ate properly these visions would go away.

Help me when I speak out and speak the truth to defend you to have the courage she had, even in the face of people who laugh at me. But let me also speak with care and love, remembering your love and care for all people.

❖ Lord Jesus, let my heart never rest until it finds you who are its centre, its love and its happiness.

By the wound in your heart pardon the sins I have committed whether out of malice or evil desires.

Place my weak heart in your divine heart, continually under your protection and guidance, so that I may persevere in doing good and in fleeing evil until my last breath. Amen
(St Margaret Mary)

I ask you especially for *[here name your intention]*

Our Father - Hail Mary - Glory Be

My God, I offer you all my prayers, works, joy, and sufferings in union with the Sacred Heart of Jesus, for the intentions for which he pleads and offers himself in the holy sacrifice of the Mass, in thanksgiving for your favours, in reparation for my sins, and in humble supplication for my temporal and eternal welfare, for the needs of our holy Mother the Church, for the conversion of sinners, and for the relief of the poor souls in purgatory.

Second Day

Lord, you promised through your Sacred Heart *all things needed for daily life* and *blessings on our undertakings* (1st and 5th Promises).

I ask for your blessings on my life and all that I do, but also to know that you lead me. You know what is best for me. May I always join myself to you so that I am yours and live in you. Let me recognise your hand in my life, see when you are guiding me and trust in your will for my life, knowing that all things work for good for those who love God.

❖ Lord Jesus, let my heart never rest…
I ask you especially for *[here name your intention]*

Our Father - Hail Mary - Glory Be

My God, I offer…

Third Day

Peace and blessings will be showered on the home dedicated to the Sacred Heart (2nd and 9th Promises).

May I pray and work every day for harmony and love in my home and in my family. May I be a sign to others of your love. Give me a heart like yours. Help me to love, to ask pardon, to forgive and to help others to reconcile. Let me recognise and be grateful for the times when your spirit appears in the family, and always put you at the centre.

❖ Lord Jesus, let my heart never rest…
I ask you especially for *[here name your intention]*
Our Father - Hail Mary - Glory Be
My God, I offer…

Fourth Day

You have promised *comfort in suffering* and *refuge in danger* (3rd and 4th Promises).

In any suffering and cross in my life you are there, waiting to comfort and console me. I know I can always find you if I call on you and wait to hear your voice. Help me too, to turn to you when I am in danger of sin, knowing you can break this attraction - that you can rescue me before I am lost.

❖ Lord Jesus, let my heart never rest…
I ask you especially for *[here name your intention]*
Our Father - Hail Mary - Glory Be
My God, I offer...

Fifth Day

Through your Sacred Heart you promise *mercy for sinners* (6th Promise).

I ask for mercy for my sins and for the gift of showing mercy to others. You said sinners will find your heart an ocean of mercy for those who seek it. I ask to trust in this and be truly grateful. May my gratitude for your forgiveness of my sins spill over into forgiveness for anyone who has wronged me.

❖ Lord Jesus, let my heart never rest…
I ask you especially for *[here name your intention]*
Our Father - Hail Mary - Glory Be
My God, I offer...

Sixth Day

Lord, you promise help both *for the tepid* and *for the fervent* (7th and 8th Promises).

I know I can be both of these things, but also how easily I become lukewarm in everything but especially in living as a Christian. May I rediscover the joy of your love and live my life in hope. When I live according to your will such a burden is lifted from me. You alone can give this fervour. Give me the desire to ask for it, and in my fervour give me discernment not to discourage or alienate others.

❖ Lord Jesus, let my heart never rest…
I ask you especially for *[here name your intention]*
Our Father - Hail Mary - Glory Be
My God, I offer…

Seventh Day

Through your Sacred Heart *priests will be given help to reach hearts* (10th Promise).

May I always remember to pray for priests I know. They are the head of the body that is your Church and the Evil One targets them. If it is in my power to encourage them, help me to do that. Give your priests courage in their daily lives and hope in you and in your Blessed Mother who loves them. May they not become cynical or sad, remembering that with you all things are possible. May they speak the truth in mercy and show their faith, hope and trust in you, believing you can reach all hearts.

❖ Lord Jesus, let my heart never rest…
I ask you especially for *[here name your intention]*
Our Father - Hail Mary - Glory Be
My God, I offer…

Eighth Day

Through your Sacred Heart you promise that I can have a true relationship with you (11th Promise).

Help me to wish for and accept a true relationship with you; to have love for you and to know happiness in your presence; to be able to feel you in my heart as St Margaret Mary did. Give me the grace to receive communion often, as you have asked us to and especially on the first Fridays.

❖ Lord Jesus, let my heart never rest…
I ask you especially for *[here name your intention]*
Our Father - Hail Mary - Glory Be
My God, I offer…

Ninth Day

Through your Sacred Heart you promise us your *grace at the moment of our death* (12th Promise).
I ask this grace of you and also the grace to live each day in the fulness you want to give me. May I be a person who gives life and not death. Give me especially a guard over my tongue so I do not destroy others with my words but instead show them kindness and encouragement. Help me not to fear death and not to find life purposeless, but instead to know death as a passage to eternal life.

❖ Lord Jesus, let my heart never rest…
I ask you especially for *[here name your intention]*
Our Father - Hail Mary - Glory Be
My God, I offer…

O most holy heart of Jesus, fountain of every blessing, I adore you, I love you, and with sorrow for my sins I offer you this heart of mine. Make me humble, patient, pure and wholly obedient to your will. Grant, good Jesus, that I may live in you and for you. Protect me in the midst of danger. Comfort me in my afflictions. Give me health of body, assistance in my temporal needs, your blessing on all that I do, and the grace of a holy death. Amen.

Novena Prayer to the Immaculate Heart of Mary

O most Blessed Mother, heart of love, heart of mercy, ever listening, caring, consoling, hear our prayer. As your children, we implore your intercession with Jesus your Son. We are comforted in knowing your heart is ever open to those who ask for your prayer. We entrust to your gentle care and intercession, those whom we love and who are sick or lonely or hurting. Help all of us, Holy Mother, to bear our burdens in this life until we may share eternal life and peace with God forever. Amen.

Transfiguration (6th August)

On his way to Jerusalem, Jesus goes up the mountain with Peter and John and there appears to them transfigured, in glory. This is usually reckoned to be a glimpse of the Uncreated Light, the divine presence that in the Hebrew Scriptures is called the Shekinah: that brightness which our eyes cannot bear nor our hearts conceive, but is the aboriginal nature of the Godhead, here glimpsed, and promised to us in the resurrection that, at the End, will renew our bodies too.

As well as on the feast of the Transfiguration, the high feast of summer, this Gospel is also read on the Second Sunday of Lent. This reminds us that the glory of new life that comes with Easter is born from the Cross; that we should not think that suffering is the end, or the only thing there is, but that it always points us forward to resurrection, and to the resplendent glory of a renewed creation.

To finish the novena on the feast, you should begin on 29th July; to finish on the eve of the feast, begin on 28th July.

The Gospel accounts of the Transfiguration are: *Mt* 17:1-8; *Mk* 9:2-8; *Lk* 9:28-36

First Day

In the Transfiguration heaven and earth meet, humanity and divinity, time and eternity. Give me the grace to see how powerful you are. You are master of the universe. If my prayer is not answered, it is not because you cannot do what I want but that you have a different and better plan for me.

❖ I ask you especially for *[here name your intention]*

Our Father - Hail Mary - Glory Be

Second Day

The prophet Malachi promised that Elijah would return as a sign the Messiah had arrived. Elijah and Moses appeared with Christ in his Transfiguration. Open our eyes to see how you speak to us in history and throughout our lives. You always keep your promises. Help us learn to read the signs of the times.

❖ I ask you especially for *[here name your intention]*

Our Father - Hail Mary - Glory Be

Third Day

Peter blurted out the first thing that came into his head, as we often do. Help me to keep a guard on my mouth; not to gossip or criticise; not to be hurtful or rude. Help me also to be careful if I tell other people how they should be living their lives.

❖ I ask you especially for *[here name your intention]*

Our Father - Hail Mary - Glory Be

Fourth Day

Finally, Peter said "it is good to be here". Give me the grace to be with you and to be glad to be with you, trusting you with my life; to know I am not alone in life; that you love me and have a wonderful plan for me if I trust you.

❖ I ask you especially for *[here name your intention]*

Our Father - Hail Mary - Glory Be

Fifth Day

At the Transfiguration, Jesus tried to prepare his disciples for the crucifixion. You tell us that if we want to follow you we should take up our cross, but we always hope that the cross will go away. Give me the courage to believe that you carry my cross with me and that it will not crush me.

❖ I ask you especially for *[here name your intention]*

Our Father - Hail Mary - Glory Be

Sixth Day

In the Transfiguration there is a glimpse of your glory; a glimpse of your divine nature. Give me this grace: to see your power in my life and have a desire for holiness. Help me to believe I will not lose myself if I follow your teachings.

❖ I ask you especially for *[here name your intention]*

Our Father - Hail Mary - Glory Be

Seventh Day

The disciples who saw your Transfiguration were terrified, but you told them to stand up and not to be afraid. Help me remember this. When life knocks me down and when I am afraid, help me to stand up and walk onward with you.

❖ I ask you especially for *[here name your intention]*

Our Father - Hail Mary - Glory Be

Eighth Day

Moses and Elijah are living in the presence of Christ in the Transfiguration. All who face death with faith in you will live in your presence for ever. Help us not to fear death.

❖ I ask you especially for *[here name your intention]*

Our Father - Hail Mary - Glory Be

Ninth Day

As in eternal life I will see your glory, so at the resurrection of the dead I too will be glorified. This life is only a small part of my life in you. Help me to look forward in hope to heaven and to the resurrection of the dead.

❖ I ask you especially for *[here name your intention]*

Our Father - Hail Mary - Glory Be

Assumption (15th August)

The Church has celebrated the passage of the Virgin Mary from this life to the fuller life with the Father for centuries, calling the mystery of her going-out the Dormition or Assumption. It was only formally defined as a certain truth of the Christian Faith in 1950, by Pope Pius XII, to the dismay of some non-Catholics.

This feast celebrates not just the unique role and eminence of the Virgin Mary, but also points towards the fulfilment that, please God, awaits us all. Mary, the Church declares, was assumed body and soul into heaven; our own promised life with God, this reminds us, will be one in which our physical self will play a full part. Heaven is not some ethereal fiesta of clouds and bodiless contemplation, but a life in all ways richer and fuller than, but in all ways also contiguous with, the life we live now. This is a feast of hope and promise.

To finish the novena on the feast itself, you should begin on 7th August; to finish on the eve of the feast, begin on 6th August.

First Day

Lord, we long to be able to reach out to you and to each other but original sin prevents us from risking this. Our Blessed Mother was free from this sin from the very moment of her conception. She is our model of how to live fully and entirely in your will. I pray for the grace to know your will for my life and the courage to enter into it with joy and hope.

❖ I ask you especially for *[here name your intention]*
Our Father - Hail Mary - Glory Be
Magnificat

Second Day

Mary was given the grace to become *theotokos* (Mother of God). You made yourself vulnerable, and gave yourself into her motherly care. You entrusted everything to her but still left her free. Help me to see what you have entrusted to me and to value it. Help me too to be worthy of that trust. May I learn to love and trust you as Mary did and know that this kind of communion with you is possible.

❖ I ask you especially for *[here name your intention]*
Our Father - Hail Mary - Glory Be
Magnificat

Third Day

Even in agony on the cross you thought of us. You gave your mother to John and to the whole Church. You have crowned her Queen of Heaven so that she can intercede for us. May I know Mary, who knows and loves me as a mother does; may I know her as someone who is interested in me, who wants to help and comfort me. Give me the grace to call on her help.

❖ I ask you especially for *[here name your intention]*
Our Father - Hail Mary - Glory Be
Magnificat

Fourth Day

Mary remained with the disciples, and witnessed the Resurrection, the Ascension and the descent of the Holy Spirit with them. Her love and faith helped give them strength. Everything she did was from love. St Francis de Sales said that Mary's death (or passing from this life) was in love, from love and through love; that, Father, she died of love for you. May I have this same desire to love you and my neighbour. Give me a heart that desires to perform the works of mercy.

❖ I ask you especially for *[here name your intention]*
Our Father - Hail Mary - Glory Be
Magnificat

Fifth Day

Legend says that, when Our Lady was about to depart this life, all the apostles were transported from where they were preaching the Gospel to her bedside - all except Thomas; but when he arrived too late to witness the Assumption, Our Lady dropped her belt from heaven as a sign he was not forgotten. Lord, help me to know your mother as my mother even when I am slow to love.

❖ I ask you especially for *[here name your intention]*
Our Father - Hail Mary - Glory Be
Magnificat

Sixth Day

Icons of the Dormition show Christ holding a baby which represents Mary's soul. He holds her as once she held him as a baby. Father, you have a plan for every person. No one is forgotten and you are always faithful even when we are not. You hold everything in being while still giving us free will. I know that I am safe in your love no matter what happens: that in the end all will be well.

❖ I ask you especially for *[here name your intention]*
Our Father - Hail Mary - Glory Be
Magnificat

Seventh Day

Mary was assumed into heaven body and soul. Help me to appreciate my body, given by God, and treat it with the dignity it deserves. We are part of the created order. Help me to understand what that means. Let me seek to discover the theology of the body and help me to live the fulness of my life as a Christian man or woman, embracing all that that means.

❖ I ask you especially for *[here name your intention]*
Our Father - Hail Mary - Glory Be
Magnificat

Eighth Day

Help me to know that in heaven I will be the fulness of myself. May I seek to become what you created me to be; may I see the importance of this. You love me as I am and for what you know I can become within the plan you have for me.

❖ I ask you especially for *[here name your intention]*
Our Father - Hail Mary - Glory Be
Magnificat

Ninth Day

Our Lady, Queen of Heaven, cares for us like the indulgent mother she is. Give me the grace to follow her example, and intercede with you for the needs of others. Help me to take time to pray for them and to care about their lives.

❖ I ask you especially for *[here name your intention]*

Our Father - Hail Mary - Glory Be

Magnificat

Exaltation of the Cross
(14th September)

This feast is sometimes called Holy Cross Day. It marks various events in the history of the (still surviving) relics of the True Cross, which the Church believes to be the physical remains of the cross on which Jesus was put to death.

The most important event is the finding of the Cross, in the year 326 AD, by the Empress Helena, mother of the Emperor Constantine. Only two years previously, Constantine had become sole ruler of the Roman world, something he attributed to his use of the cross as a battle sign. His victory established Christianity as the public faith of the Empire, put an end to the sporadic persecutions it had endured, and allowed the Church to emerge from its long hiding. The physical places and things that reminded Christians of the life and death of Jesus, and of his earliest followers, were now generally made known (they had often been previously concealed, either by Christians to keep them safe from the authorities, or by the authorities themselves to try and scotch the growing Christian cult).

Helena had been divorced by Constantine's father so he could make a political marriage, and had lived much of her life in comparative obscurity. Legend makes her a British princess, and there is no good reason not to believe this, although other stories about her parentage are found. At any rate, she was not of the Roman aristocracy, and was not felt to be quite the right sort of wife for an Emperor. At some stage she had become Christian. By the time her son became Emperor, she was an old woman. He quickly rehabilitated her and declared her Empress Dowager; almost her first official act was to hurry off to the Holy Land to look for the relics of the Cross. They were found, and identified, after a series of events that look like miracles.

So why does the Church make such a fuss about what are, after all, just some old pieces of wood?

One reason is that the relics of the Cross anchor the Christian story firmly in history. Unlike the other mystery religions popular in the late Roman Empire (and their "new age" analogues today), the Church insists that the great drama of human salvation - the events that show us that God is, indisputably and irrevocably, on our side - issues from a series of historical occurrences, which have left tangible remains we can still see and touch.

Secondly, the Cross of Jesus Christ, which is the fulcrum of human history, is also the pattern of all the crosses we ourselves experience: those sometimes agonisingly painful events that God sends us, not to punish us or discourage or destroy us, but to allow us to enter the mystery of suffering - so we may know in our own lives the frankly incredible paradox that these appalling things are the very means by which God shows his love for us, and allows us to rise above our sins and selfishnesses. The Cross - Jesus's Cross, but our cross also - is the means by which the world is saved, is brought to know God's love. This is at first sight a baffling and even offensive notion; how dare the professionally religious talk to us in such a way? Even on reflection, the teaching is almost impossibly hard to accept. So we need to put it before God, honestly, in our prayer. We need to ask him to show us, to help us truly and really to know and feel, that our cross - those sufferings from which we most desire to escape - is in fact the sign and the instrument of the love that the Father has for us. Reasoned argument will not do this; prayer can.

To finish the novena on the eve of the feast, you should begin on 5th September; to finish on the feast itself, begin on 6th September.

First Day

The Roman Emperor Hadrian wanted to obliterate all signs of Christianity in Jerusalem, but in doing this he actually marked the places and preserved the relics. Even the things that seem to be absolutely against my interests can end up being the best thing for me. Give me, Lord, the grace to trust in your wisdom.

❖ Help me to see the cross in my life and to embrace it.
I ask you especially for *[here name your intention]*

Our Father - Hail Mary - Glory Be

We adore you, O Christ, and praise you because by your Holy Cross you have redeemed the world.

Second Day

Legend says that when St Helena's team found the Cross, they in fact found three crosses. Nobody could tell which was the True Cross until a sick woman was brought to the place. When she touched the True Cross she was cured. Help me to discern in my life what things I should try to fight against and what is my true cross.

❖ Help me to see the cross in my life and to embrace it.
I ask you especially for *[here name your intention]*

Our Father - Hail Mary - Glory Be

We adore you, O Christ, and praise you because by your Holy Cross you have redeemed the world.

Third Day

St Helena was old when she set out to find the Cross and had suffered many injustices in her life, but she did not let that dull her faith or make her bitter. St Ambrose said that when Helena found the True Cross she did not worship the Cross itself but "him who hung on that wood. She burned with an earnest desire to touch the guarantee of immortality." Give me the grace of a deep faith like hers.

❖ Help me to see the cross in my life and to embrace it.
I ask you especially for *[here name your intention]*

Our Father - Hail Mary - Glory Be

We adore you, O Christ, and praise you because by your Holy Cross you have redeemed the world.

Fourth Day

The Protestant John Calvin said there were enough alleged pieces of the True Cross to fill a ship as he scoffed at the faith of the Church. In the nineteenth century this jibe was proved untrue: a French architect, Charles Rohault de Fleury, measured all the surviving fragments and determined they would together make up only a small part of a cross. However, pieces of the Cross were sent all over the world. They are a sign of your kingship throughout the world. Give me the grace to know your power.

❖ Help me to see the cross in my life and to embrace it.
I ask you especially for *[here name your intention]*

Our Father - Hail Mary - Glory Be

We adore you, O Christ, and praise you because by your Holy Cross you have redeemed the world.

Fifth Day

You have said that those who wish to follow you must pick up their cross every day. Give me the discernment to see that if I embrace my cross you also carry it. Give me the grace to enter the life you give me, not sadly or bitterly but in hope.

❖ Help me to see the cross in my life and to embrace it. I ask you especially for *[here name your intention]*

Our Father - Hail Mary - Glory Be

We adore you, O Christ, and praise you because by your Holy Cross you have redeemed the world.

Sixth Day

It is hard to understand suffering and especially the suffering of those I love. Help me to see that you love them more than I do, and to trust you with their lives. Give me the grace to help them but not to try to take away their crosses, which are their only way to you.

❖ Help me to see the cross in my life and to embrace it. I ask you especially for *[here name your intention]*

Our Father - Hail Mary - Glory Be

We adore you, O Christ, and praise you because by your Holy Cross you have redeemed the world.

Seventh Day

You showed your love by going to the Cross, by suffering, by offering up your life. Help me to see what I can do to follow you. Give me the gift of Christian love. Help me to be open to others and to offer up my suffering for the world, not forcing myself but allowing you to show me how to give.

❖ Help me to see the cross in my life and to embrace it. I ask you especially for *[here name your intention]*

Our Father - Hail Mary - Glory Be

We adore you, O Christ, and praise you because by your Holy Cross you have redeemed the world.

Eighth Day

Help me truly believe that you love me so much you died for me. You love me, as the person that I am. You see me and you still love me. This love cannot be measured. You love me more than I can imagine and even though you love all people, you still love me as though I were the only one. Help me to believe and rejoice in that love.

❖ Help me to see the cross in my life and to embrace it. I ask you especially for *[here name your intention]*

Our Father - Hail Mary - Glory Be

We adore you, O Christ, and praise you because by your Holy Cross you have redeemed the world.

Ninth Day

When you were on earth everyone thought you would conquer with power, but instead you took the last place. You allowed all humiliations and evil to attack you. You accepted hatred and violence and still love us. Help me understand this. I don't look for masochism but for humility; to be able to pass through suffering, knowing that if I follow you I too will overcome death.

❖ Help me to see the cross in my life and to embrace it. I ask you especially for *[here name your intention]*

Our Father - Hail Mary - Glory Be

We adore you, O Christ, and praise you because by your Holy Cross you have redeemed the world.

Christ the King

If Jesus Christ is a king, his kingdom, as he declares to Pilate, is not of this world. The Kingdom of God is not

some theocratic state to be achieved by force of arms and a clericalised polity, as some in the past have thought. Insofar as God's kingdom is visibly present in the world, it is that thing we call the Church. But it is not by any means confined to the

obvious and outward structures of the Church, although we have Jesus's assurance that the Spirit will not wholly abandon these. Outside these visible things, God is always present to his people, and acts by means we cannot see or know, except by the clear evidence of love shown and suffering accepted: of love that is stronger than death. This is the sign of God's kingdom. Any who bear this token are in some sense subjects of Christ the King. But he is a king who rules by mercy and by forgiveness. It is not for us to be jealous of his mercy to those whom we do not recognise as our fellow-subjects, or our fellow-Christians. It is enough that we ask his mercy for ourselves, and for the world.

The feast of Christ the King is celebrated on the last Sunday of the Church's year, before the start of Advent and at the end of Ordinary Time. To end on the feast, begin the novena on the Saturday before the preceding Sunday; to end on the eve of the feast, begin on the Friday of that week.

For the feast of Christ the King, the Church assigns three different Gospels, one for each year of the Sunday cycle (A, B and C). They are *Mt* 25:31-46 (A); *Jn* 18:33-37 (B); *Lk* 23:35-43 (C).

First Day

Mt 25:31-46

This Gospel is a parable of the End of Days. The citizens of the kingdom are the merciful. This is the sole criterion - not how hard or profoundly we have prayed, or how much we have fasted or denied ourselves; but how far we have shown mercy to those in need.

❖ Father, help me to be merciful.
I ask you especially for *[here name your intention]*
Our Father - Hail Mary - Glory Be

Second Day

Mt 25:31-46

The Gospel is very clear that we need to consider all those we meet who require our help as, in effect, bearers of Jesus Christ.

Christ is in each person; this is another reason to show love to them, apart from their dignity as human beings made in God's image (although these facts are closely related).

❖ I ask you especially for *[here name your intention]*
Our Father - Hail Mary - Glory Be

Third Day

Mt 25:31-46

The King here acts as judge; but the judgement is not based on an abstract law, but born of his own relationship with the one on trial. "How did you behave to me?" is his question. We should not get tied up in nice questions about whether whatever instances we can allege where we did show mercy to others will somehow outweigh the countless occasions we have shown neglect; but rather try to see how, on this day, at this moment, I can be merciful and not neglectful to whichever of my neighbours is in need.

❖ Father, help me to live in the present moment and not be imprisoned by my past sins.
I ask you especially for *[here name your intention]*
Our Father - Hail Mary - Glory Be

Fourth Day

Jn 18:33-37

It is hard not to feel some sympathy for Pilate here, at least as John presents him. The harassed colonial administrator trying to keep the peace between squabbling native holy men is not perhaps so immediately sympathetic a figure for us as he was to our grandparents' generation, but we can recognise, surely, a picture of a man trying to judge fairly a quarrel that is not his own, that he does not understand, and that frankly rather bores him, except for the nagging danger that it will provoke a riot, with all the tiresome complications of destruction of property and disruption to commerce, bother and injury to the garrison, and writing reports about it all to Rome. It was also good Roman practice to keep claimants to native kingdoms alive and compliant, in case a figurehead for a new regime was needed.

Pilate's misfortune was to be caught up in something he did not understand, and for which his standard battery of responses was simply inadequate.

Sometimes we find ourselves similarly out of our depth; we need to be careful not to be led astray by fear or expediency.

❖ Father, help me to see things as you see them, and not be swayed by fear or self-interest at the expense of mercy. I ask you especially for *[here name your intention]*

Our Father - Hail Mary - Glory Be

Fifth Day

Jn 18:33-37

After much prompting, Jesus tells Pilate, "Mine is not a kingdom of this world". Pilate humours him; this is probably some species of harmless lunatic, with perhaps a certain way with words, who has got caught up in a piece of Temple politics. No need to make a fuss; flog him for his pains, and send him on his way. As we know, the religious authorities weren't willing to let the matter drop so easily, and Pilate gave in to their nagging. But his first reaction is not untypical. Many people today see religion as a harmless eccentricity, to be tolerated as long as it doesn't make a fuss or try to pretend it has anything to do with the serious business of getting on with life. We can be tempted to go along with this estimation: to avoid doing or saying anything that might be embarrassing.

❖ Father, help me not to pretend things don't matter for the sake of a quiet life.
I ask you especially for *[here name your intention]*
Our Father - Hail Mary - Glory Be

Sixth Day

Jn 18:33-37

Jesus's kingdom is founded on truth, not on violence or power or political accommodation. This is an irrelevance to Pilate, as to most lazily practical men: he famously responds, "What is truth?" But "all who are on the side of truth" listen to Jesus's voice. What does it mean, to be on the side of truth? One thing it means, perhaps, is trying to live in honesty, speaking truthfully to others and hearing the truth about ourselves without reflexively defending ourselves against anything that challenges our self-delusion. It means trying to live honestly and openly, without taking refuge behind masks and conventional pieties.

We see in Jesus how the world treats those who bear witness to the truth; but we know, too, that he himself will be with those who listen to his voice.

❖ Father, help me not to be afraid of or indifferent to the truth; help me to speak the truth in love, and hear it without fear.

I ask you especially for *[here name your intention]*

Our Father - Hail Mary - Glory Be

Seventh Day

Lk 23:35-43

Now the King is crucified: helpless, naked and a spectacle to be mocked. Let us not suppose we would be slow to join in the mockery; most of us, if we are honest, take some pleasure in seeing the humiliation of the hitherto popular and successful, and these things are infectious. It is a poor sort of king, by all normal standards, who ends up pinned on a gibbet by the roadside. This, though, is how human beings react to the love of the merciful Father; and his answer is, always, forgiveness.

❖ Father, help me not to delight in others' misfortune.
I ask you especially for *[here name your intention]*
Our Father - Hail Mary - Glory Be

Eighth Day

Lk 23:35-43

If you are a king, then why don't you save yourself? This question is put to Jesus by the Jewish leaders, by the soldiers of the crucifixion party and even by one of the criminals crucified with him. This is certainly not the model of heroic leadership our culture is comfortable with; a Hollywood script would have Jesus rescued by his disciples, who had somehow found courage they never knew they had, or, perhaps, wrenching himself free from his cross in an access of hitherto latent super-strength, scattering Roman soldiers like matchsticks. Or something like that. We do not like our heroes to be defeated. It seems unlikely that Jesus's contemporaries, reared on stories of the glorious victories of the Maccabees, would have been much different.

But this is what Christ's kingship looks like; and what, in the world's eyes, his followers have to look forward to. But beyond this defeat, this disappointment, is something of an altogether different order: victory over death, a victory that, unlike those of earthly kings, can never be overturned or undone.

❖ Father, help me not to reckon success and failure as the world does.

I ask you especially for *[here name your intention]*

Our Father - Hail Mary - Glory Be

Ninth Day

Lk 23:35-43

We should have no doubt that the men crucified with Jesus were villains; one of them admits as much. By the crude standards of the day, they got what they deserved. And yet one of them turns to Jesus (and repentance, remember, means literally a turning towards God) and asks to be remembered by Jesus when he comes into his kingdom. He is at once given a promise that he will join him in paradise. God's mercy is like this, this Gospel says. What matters is not what we have done, or how often, but that we ask to be forgiven.

❖ Father, forgive me my sins; call me into your kingdom.

I ask you especially for *[here name your intention]*

Our Father - Hail Mary - Glory Be

Handbook of Novenas to the Saints
Short Prayers for Needs & Graces

This booklet contains newly composed novena prayers asking for the intercession of various saints. The long experience of praying Christians, and the teaching of the Church, assure us that the duty of Christians to support each other with prayer does not end with this life, and the saints delight to add their voices to ours when we make our requests to God our Father. Each novena is prefaced with a short biography of the saint, which gives some suggestions of the particular intentions or needs where their intercession has been found especially powerful.

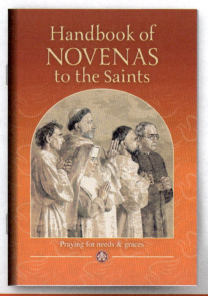

A Handbook of Scriptural Novenas
For Various Needs and Intentions

These newly composed novena prayers present figures from Scripture from whom we learn lessons in faith and prayer. The situations and difficulties they faced frequently mirror our own worries and concerns. Thus Hannah prays for the gift of children, Job learns to be honest with God, Martha complains that she does all the work, Deborah and Barak learn what to do when overwhelmed, and Jonah too when God's plan doesn't seem to make sense. These and other figures open the Scriptures to us, and we learn more of the Novenas as a form of prayer.

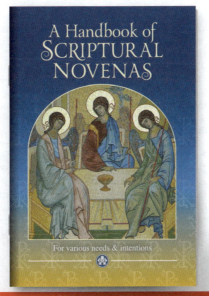

Picture credits

Page 8, *John the Baptist*. Mosaic from the Hagia Sophia church, Istanbul, Turkey. © PavleMarjanovic/Shutterstock.com. Page 16, *Detail of the painting of Our Lady Immaculate*. Sicily, Italy. © Fotogiunta/Shutterstock.com. Page 20, *Stained glass window depicting Nativity Scene*. Cathedral of Brussels. © Jorisvo/Shutterstock.com. Page 28, *Stained glass window depicting the birth of Jesus Christ, with Mary and the Magi*. Ely Cathedral, UK. © Olan/Shutterstock.com. Page 38, *The Fresco of Annunciation*. Facade of Metropolitan Cathedral. By B. Antoniasis, 1895. Athens, Greece. © Renata Sedmakova/Shutterstock.com. Page 46, *Lamb of God*. Neo-gothic Stained-glass window. Matthias Church, Budapest, Hungary. © Zomby/Shutterstock.com. Page 55, *Stained glass window depicting the Holy Spirit Dove*. © Nancy Bauer/Shutterstock.com. Page 60, *Stained glass window depicting Sacred Heart of Jesus*. © Nancy Bauer/Shutterstock.com. Page 68, *Fresco of the Transfiguration of Jesus*. St Constanstine and Helena orthodox church. © Renata Sedmakova/Shutterstock.com. Page 72, *Assumption of the Virgin Mary*. © Zvonimir Atletic/Shutterstock.com. Page 78, *Stained glass portrait of Jesus*. © CURAphotography/Shutterstock.com. Page 86, *Crown & Cross* Stained glass window. © GWImages/Shutterstock.com.